Swarthmore Lecture 1975

Margaret Brooks-graton

THE SENSE OF GLORY:

a psychological study
of peak-experiences

by Ralph Hetherington

FHSC

FRIENDS HOME SERVICE COMMITTEE·LONDON

First published May 1975

© Ralph Hetherington
Friends Home Service Committee
Friends House, Euston Road, London, NW1 2BJ

ISBN 0 85245 117 2

Cover design by John Blamires

*Painting on front cover reproduced
by courtesy of the Trustees,
The National Gallery, London*

*Printed in Great Britain in 10/12 Times
By Headley Brothers Ltd., 109 Kingsway,
London, WC2B 6PX and Ashford, Kent*

PREFACE

The Swarthmore Lectureship was established
by the Woodbrooke Extension Committee at a
meeting held December 9th, 1907: the minute
of the Committee providing for 'an annual
lecture on some subject relating to the message
and work of the Society of Friends'. The name
Swarthmore was chosen in memory of the
home of Margaret Fox, which was always open
to the earnest seeker after Truth, and from
which loving words of sympathy and
substantial material help were sent to fellow
workers.

The lectureship has a twofold purpose; first, to
interpret further to the members of the Society
of Friends their message and mission; and,
secondly, to bring before the public the spirit,
the aims and fundamental principles of the
Friends. The lecturer alone is responsible for
any opinions expressed.

The Lectures have usually been delivered at the
time of assembly of London Yearly Meeting
of the Society of Friends. The present Lecture
in abridged form, was delivered at Friends House,
Euston Road, London, on the evening of
May 25th, 1975.

In 1966 the Friends Home Service Committee
took over the publication of the Swarthmore
Lectures from George Allen & Unwin Ltd., who
had published them for many years.

THE PICTURE ON THE COVER

The picture on the cover,* known as 'The Ambassadors',
was painted by Hans Holbein, the Younger, in 1533. It is
particularly relevant in ways which I hope will become
evident as this essay is read.

It shows two men in a room, surrounded by objects of many
different kinds. The picture is intensely realistic: painted
life-size, in great detail like a coloured photograph in sharp
focus although the impression is somehow more realistic
than a photograph. The emphasis too is on instantaneity, the
present moment, the here and now. The year, date and hour
of the scene are all recorded in the picture. Yet at the same
time, the youth and vigour of the two figures, so
accurately set in time and space, are depicted alongside
conventional symbols of death: the crucifix, the broken
lute, and, most disquieting of all, the distorted skull on the
floor: out of space, rather than out of time.

The figures themselves are sharply contrasted. The worldly,
dashing, extraverted figure on the left, and the quiet,
withdrawn, introverted figure on the right. The practical
man of action is contrasted with the contemplative.

The momentary experience or timeless moment, the
concentration of attention leading to detailed awareness
of the scene, and the contrast between practical action
and passive contemplation; are all themes which form
integral parts of the subject matter of this essay.

*Reproduced by courtesy of the Trustees, The National
Gallery, London.

FOREWORD

When I had recovered from my astonishment at being asked to write a Swarthmore lecture, I was surprised all over again to discover that I knew what I was going to write about. It had seemed to me for a long time that, while Friends have always emphasized the importance of firsthand religious experience, it had never been tackled head-on, as it were, as a topic in its own right. To use today's fashionable term, it had never been tackled phenomenologically. It is true, of course, that the concept of the 'Inward Light' has been central to Friends' thinking, and many books and articles have been written about it. Yet there has never been, to my knowledge, any attempt by Friends to discuss the thing itself in every day experiential terms, and to relate it to Friends' way of worship. What is it like to have a religious experience? How does it differ from other kinds of experience? Do such experiences lead anywhere? Do they have any practical results?

This I knew would be my topic. But how to tackle it? Here again there was no hesitation. Since I had been trained as a professional psychologist it must be from this point of view for better or worse that the analysis must be made.

The sources of my views are largely evident from the references to books referred to throughout the text. However, I should like to also pay tribute to C. V. Stuart Payne about whom David Wills wrote in *The Friend* on 17th August 1973. Stuart had a powerful influence on my thinking as a young man during the War. Another Friend who greatly influenced my psychological thinking was John C. Raven with whom I did my clinical training. Although John wrote little himself his influence as a teacher was profound.

Dorothy Hetherington has contributed to the development of the essay at every stage. Julie Hetherington and Robert Tod read an early version of the manuscript and made many suggestions which led to considerable modifications of the text. In paying tribute to all the help I have received, I must nevertheless accept sole responsibility for all that I have written.

My thanks are due to the University of Liverpool who allowed me to spend my 1974 University month on the essay.

Highgate, January, 1975

At certain moments the individual is carried beyond his rational self on to another ethical plane where his actions are judged by new standards. The impulse which moves him to irrational action I have called the sense of glory.

Herbert Read

CONTENTS

INTRODUCTION

A sudden concentration of attention on a rainy August morning. Clusters of bright red berries, some wrinkled, some blemished, others perfect, hanging among green leaves. Drops of rain glistening on berries and leaves. The experience could not have lasted more than a few seconds, but that was a moment out of time. I was caught up in what I saw, I became part of it: the berries, the leaves, the raindrops and I, we were all of a piece. A moment of beauty and harmony and meaning. A moment of understanding.

This personal experience is an example of what I shall later refer to as being-cognition. The present essay is concerned with paying attention, not only to our surroundings, to the outer world of sense; but also to the inner world of thoughts, images, memories, fantasies and dreams. When we pay attention in the appropriate way, we may begin to be aware of people, things, ideas and images in a rather different way, so that we enter a new dimension of experience. This added dimension Herbert Read[1] has called the sense of glory. Such experiences may be highly charged with emotion and feeling, and this may motivate us to later action.

In discussing these different dimensions of awareness, it will be convenient to use some descriptive terms which may be new to some readers. These are Robert Ornstein's *non-linear consciousness*, as against linear consciousness, and Abraham Maslow's *being-cognition* as against what he calls our everyday deficiency-cognition. Occasionally either or both non-linear consciousness and being-cognition may lead to what Maslow calls *peak-experiences*. I have introduced these terms now, so that readers can be prepared for them when they meet them in the text. I shall further explain what is meant by these terms when I come to use them.

The particular group of experiences which include religious experiences, are notoriously difficult to describe. But they can sometimes be communicated poetically when the poet uses words which evoke emotions in his readers more telling than any bald description. Such experiences are ephemeral, momentary, difficult to pin down in an exact form of words. If we try to do so, they may lose their essential quality of life, like a butterfly pinned to a board. Moreover, many readers may resent having their most precious experiences and deepest feelings probed and analysed in this way.

Yet, unless such an analysis is attempted, and a description, however inadequate, is made, we are not so likely to understand what it is we seek, or even, possibly, to recognize that we are beginning to find it, when such experiences come our way.

This essay begins with a description of how we become aware of ourselves as being separate from our surroundings, and thus able to experience events as happening outside ourselves. All our memories of these events and our thoughts about them, make up the inner world of ideas, fantasies, and dreams.

I shall then describe the way in which we become aware of the sticks, stones and people in our surroundings, and how this awareness is modified by our own pattern of needs which provide, as it were, a set of blinkers preventing us from noticing some things, and forcing us to pay attention to others. I shall then give some examples of peak-experiences, and relate these to meditation and worship. Finally I shall discuss the relevance of these experiences to action.

This rather cold-blooded analysis of intimate personal and group experiences is not out of line with the Quaker tradition of openness to empirical enquiry. Not for nothing have scientists like Dalton, Lister, Eddington and Lonsdale been members of the Society of Friends. Quakers will be familiar with George Fox's dilemma as a young man when he found that various religious authorities disagreed about creeds and the interpretation of scripture. He described his experiences thus:

> For I saw there was none among them all that could speak to my condition. And when all my hopes in them and in all men were gone, so that I had nothing outwardly to help me, nor could tell what to do, then, Oh then, I heard a voice which said, 'There is one, even Christ Jesus, that can speak to thy condition', and when I heard it my heart did leap for joy.[2]

In the last analysis, he realized, enlightenment could only come from personal, empirical experience. Later he was to say, in a famous sermon at Ulverston Church, 'You will say, Christ saith this, and the apostles say this; but what canst thou say?'

This essay attempts to answer just that question.

THE SELF AND AWARENESS

In normal circumstances, the mature adult human being is able to distinguish clearly between the outer world of sticks and stones and people and all that is going on around him, and the inner world of thoughts, ideas, memories, fantasies and dreams. If this ability to distinguish between the two kinds of experience becomes impaired so that he takes his fantasies for real, then he is said to be hallucinated and may be considered insane. While we are dreaming, of course, we may certainly take our fantasies for real. This fact greatly disturbed Descartes and led him to his famous statement *cogito ergo sum*: I think therefore I exist. However, we realize, once we wake up, that we have been dreaming. Indeed, the dreamer sometimes knows that he is dreaming at the time, although this is not usually the case.

The ability to distinguish between inner and outer experiences implies that we have achieved self-awareness. Indeed, the very idea of awareness implies that there must be something which is aware of something else: the writer of his pen, the dreamer of his dream. However this separateness between the experiencer and the thing he experiences comes about only after a long process of learning on the part of the infant and young child, leading to self-awareness.

The development of the self
The human infant seems to have no experience of himself as a separate identity. He seems to have experiences of pleasure

which he learns can be repeated or prolonged by certain actions on his part, and to have other experiences of an unpleasant kind which he learns can be terminated by certain other actions. Thus when he is uncomfortable or in pain, he soon learns that crying brings the comfort of an adult's attention, and that cooing or gurgling may prolong that attention. It is only when he is about six months old that he has matured sufficiently and has had enough experience of life to begin to distinguish his mother or nurse from other people, and to recognize familiar faces from strange ones. Only when he can discriminate in this way is he able to begin to relate to other people as individuals and to begin to experience himself as an individual. During those early months he has been learning about himself, gradually accumulating experience about his own body and about inanimate objects. If he touches his left hand with his right, he feels one hand with the other, and the other with the one. When he touches the blanket there is a single tactile experience only. We have only to touch an arm or leg in bed when it has become temporarily numb, to realize the difference between a two-point and a one-point contact. The anaesthetized limb feels like an alien object, when normally it is experienced as very much part of ourselves. Thus the infant begins to discover that his body is somehow different from other objects and is the source of special experiences. He learns, too, that his body has limits, that it stretches out only so far into space, and that it is only his body that gives rise to experiences of heat and cold, touch and pain. His mother's handling of him, the stroking, patting and general massage of his body surfaces are all powerful sources of stimulation which teach him the size and shape of his body, and develop what is known as his 'body image'. Lack of mothering at this early stage may retard the infant's development, and seriously impede the child's growing sense of his identity. Babies who have been

6

denied this early mothering grow up grossly retarded, inert, speechless and unresponsive.

Probably by the end of the first year, the child has found his place in, and realized his physical separateness from, the world outside his body. The child's body, being the source of sensations and therefore the means whereby contact is made with the outside world, becomes firmly the seat of the experienced self. The young child will also find he has wants which conflict with other people's wants, and so begins also to be aware of himself as a wanter as well as an experiencer.

Extreme emotional dependence on the mother or other familiar adults usually lasts until the child is about three years of age. Until then the child is unable to tolerate separation from the mother or other familiar adults, for any long period without acute distress. When such separation does occur the child may first become angry, then terrified and finally apathetic or depressed. When he is finally reunited with his family, it may take weeks or months for his relationship with them to return to normal. After the age of three, he is usually sufficiently emotionally independent to be able to tolerate separation without these extreme reactions. The child or young person will continue to show some emotional dependence on his family for another fifteen or twenty years. During the first quarter century of life, the growing individual has to achieve a separate identity: a concept and realization of himself not only as physically separate from his surroundings, but as someone with a place in the world, who knows his way around, what he wants and how to achieve it, what he can reasonably expect to attain, and what he must learn to do without. He has to discover himself as a unique and recognizable personality.

This long struggle for a separate identity can only be successfully completed by constant interplay between the individual and his surroundings and between the individual and other individuals. Blind and deaf children, or children born with motor handicaps which impair mobility, nearly always develop more slowly and with greater difficulty than normal children. People with mental illnesses that impair contact with others often complain of depersonalization or loss of identity. Some research has been done which has involved depriving normal volunteer subjects of nearly all sensory stimulation by enclosing them in dark soundproof rooms. After some time, which varies with different people, they become confused, cannot think rationally, and may even become deluded and hallucinated. They lose all clear sense of self and of their orientation in time and space. It appears from this, that we need close and continual contact with people and things, not only to develop properly, but also to remain sane and on an even keel. There are, of course, individual exceptions. Some people seem to thrive on a hermit-like existence, largely remote from others without becoming unbalanced. Indeed, there are plenty of records of unusual people who have lived as hermits and achieved strikingly advanced levels of personality development. But such people were already well integrated with stable and developed personalities before they sought seclusion. Moreover their seclusion was probably by no means total, in that they had frequent periods when they met and talked with others; or the seclusion was of limited duration, usually in preparation for some special task ahead.

Internal and external awareness

At the beginning of this chapter, I included in the range of experiences of which the self is aware, not only the external world of sticks and stones and people, but also the internal world of ideas, images, memories and dreams. Moreover I pointed out that in normal circumstances the individual is able to distinguish between those experiences which come from his surroundings, and those which are internal.

It is now important to note that these internal experiences are directly related to, and indeed arise from, prior experience of the external world. A man who has been blind from birth, for example, cannot imagine what colour can be like, nor what it would be like to experience visual shape. A congenitally blind man has no visual imagery just as a congenitally deaf person has no imagery of music or the spoken word.

The raw material of thinking, imagery, dreams and fantasies, therefore, must come from firsthand empirical experience of the external world. External experience has a 'givenness' about it which is unmistakable. The patterning, re-arrangement and re-ordering of these experiences or the memories of them, and the images and fantasies based on them are the sources of insight, inspiration and originality which come to us from time to time. The newness, freshness and unexpectedness of these insights also have a 'givenness' about them. But this lies in the patterning of the ideas, which are themselves still derived from external experience. There is, indeed, nothing new under the sun, but there are infinite possibilities of original ideas based on old experiences. An often quoted example is that of Einstein, who did no experiments, used no data not well known to many others, yet reordered them to produce a totally new idea.

John Locke was the first to propound the principle that there are no innate ideas. Aveling puts Locke's principle very clearly as follows:

> It may be laid down as a general principle which admits of no exception whatever that all data for belief, even if this be of a most elaborate philosophical or scientific character, are directly derived by us from our own immediate empirical experience or else are in some quite definite and ascertainable way related to it.[3]

2

In the same way there is no evidence that man has an instinct to believe in God, or that such belief is intuitive or comes from some special sort of revelation. If he believes in God, it must be because he perceives, or responds to, external events in such a way that belief in God is a reasonable inference from such perception or response. As Alistair Kee puts it, 'There is no direct experience of God, only experiences which are interpreted in a religious manner.'[4] John Macmurray has put this point as follows:

Science has its facts from which all hypotheses, constructions and laws are derived and to which they refer. These facts are ordinary data of universal human experience. The field of science is the whole body of common fact which it is the scientist's endeavour to understand. Religion, also, must have its ground and starting point in facts of human experience. If it conceives another world than this and asserts its existence and so passes altogether beyond the limits of our experience in this world, it can only be because there are certain elements in our common experience of this world which constrain it to do so.[5]

Our intimations of immortality are sometimes derived directly from our experience of the external world. The paradigm of this source of religious experience is that of Moses:

Moses was minding the flock of his father-in-law Jethro, priest of Midian. He led the flock along the side of the wilderness and came to Horeb, the mountain of God. There the angel of the Lord appeared to him in the flame of a burning bush. Moses noticed that, although the bush was on fire, it was not being burned up; so he said to himself, 'I must go across and see this wonderful sight. Why does not the bush burn away?' When the Lord saw that Moses had turned aside to look, he called to him out of the bush, 'Moses, Moses.' And Moses answered, 'Yes, I am here.' God said, 'Come no nearer; take off your sandals; the place where you are standing is holy ground.'[6]

More often, perhaps, we find the source of religious experience in our inner world of thoughts, ideas and feelings. The Quaker concept of the Inward Light; the quiet, inward looking nature of Quaker meeting for worship, the common practice of inward prayer and meditation involving a withdrawal from the outward world of sense; are all examples of this. One of the best descriptions of this approach has been made by Thomas Kelly in his essay on prayer in *Reality of the Spiritual World*.

> This practice of continuous prayer in the presence of God involves developing the habit of carrying on the mental life at two levels. At one level we are immersed in this world of time, of daily affairs. At the same time, but at a deeper level of our minds, we are in active relation with the Eternal Life.[7]

From this it seems that both our external experience of the world about us, and our internal experiences can be fruitful sources of religious experience. But, as we have seen, our internal experiences are derived from our external awareness of the world around us.

It must follow from this that it will be important to understand how we become aware of our surroundings, and this I shall discuss in the next chapter.

II

STICKS, STONES AND PEOPLE

Sensory experience

Our knowledge of our surroundings is obtained by means of
sense organs at or near the surface of the body: eyes, ears, nose,
tongue and also the skin, which contains nerve endings which
react to touch, temperature and pressure. Other clues are
gained from such structures as the semi-circular canals in the
ear which tell us if we are changing our orientation in the
gravitational field. However, each sense organ can be stimulated
only by its own particular form of energy: the eye by electromagnetic waves, the ear by variations in air pressure, the nose
by chemical stimuli and so on. We cannot see smells or taste
sounds. Moreover, each sense organ is capable of responding
only to a minute range of its own specific stimulus. Thus
although the electromagnetic spectrum ranges in wavelength
from less than one billionth of a metre with cosmic rays to
more than a thousand metres with radio waves, the eye can
respond only to a tiny fraction of this range between 400 and
700 billionths of a metre. In the same way we can hear sounds
only within a limited frequency range. Dogs, for example,
react to pitches which are too high for men to hear: a fact of
which poachers have taken advantage in their use of very
high pitched whistles by means of which they can call their
dogs without alerting the gamekeeper.

Arthur Eddington in *The Nature of the Physical World*[8]
points out that the solid, coloured, shaped, familiar table at
which we write or have our meals, consists at the atomic level

largely of empty space occupied by bundles of energy at enormous distances from each other, relative to their size. Thus our table viewed from the sub-atomic scale would be quite unrecognizable. Equally if we viewed it from the supra-galactic scale, it would disappear as a separate entity. If we changed the time scale, the world would appear very different. A plant can be photographed every six hours, and the stills put through a cine-projector. When this is done, thus speeding up the time scale, the growing plant visibly expands, its shoots appearing to move purposefully seeking the light, or finding other things to attach themselves to. It looks and behaves very much like an animal.

Our particular view of the world is therefore constrained by the temporal and spatial scales in which we experience it. This experience of what is going on is thus only one particular version made possible for us by the design and functioning of our brains and sense organs. Many other versions would be possible were we to operate in different scales of time and space, and were our sense organs sensitive to different ranges of energy. Moreover, the electromagnetic energy impinging on our eyes is not itself coloured: it is the eye and the brain which, as it were, turn it into perceived colour; just as the ears and the brain turn silent sound waves into perceived noises.

Thus our brains and sense organs select the range of sensations from which we build our awareness of the world around us. This discrimination between the enormous number of possible stimuli to which we might have become sensitive, probably came about by natural selection, so that we have become sensitive to just those stimuli which are necessary for survival. From these stimuli we have been able to construct a stable consciousness which amounts to the best guess we can make about what the world may really be like. Indeed were we sensitive to the full range of energy forms impinging on us from our external environment, we should become utterly confused by a great deal of irrelevant and useless information. Aldous Huxley in *The Doors of Perception*[9] writes of the measly trickle of information of which we are actually aware, and suggests that in certain circumstances we might be able to increase our range of sensitivity. This is what he means when he writes about 'cleansed perception' which people are able to achieve in certain mental states when they apparently become aware of features of their environment of which they were previously unaware. However this is probably because they have overcome some *psychological* barriers to full perception, rather than because their sense organs have become more sensitive. It is these psychological barriers that I discuss in the next sections.

We have to learn to experience the world as we do

Each sense organ provides us with a special experience quite different from those provided by other sense organs. We do not confuse sights with sounds, and both are quite different from smells. Nevertheless, we are not constantly aware of these separate experiences; we do not say, 'Now I am seeing, now I am hearing' and so on. We are usually aware of a total perceptual experience. 'Now I am talking to John and he is telling me about his holiday in Spain'; 'Now I am out shopping in the High Street and had better wait for this lorry to pass before I cross the road.' One psychologist put this well when he said that we look out of the window and say 'It's going to rain'; we do not say 'My visual field is mottled blue and grey'. In other words, we are aware of our sensations already interpreted, combined, and organized into meaningful experiences, often of a highly complex nature. All this has to be learned. Since people have somewhat different learning experiences, each person will experience the world rather differently, so that every one of us lives in his own unique

15

perceptual world, never quite the same as anyone else's. The more we differ in age, cultural or educational background, the more will our perceptual worlds differ.

We only notice what interests us or is important to us

When we are cheerful and optimistic we tend to notice the pleasant and beautiful; when we are unhappy and pessimistic we tend to notice the dreary and ugly features of our surroundings. This capacity of us all to respond to certain features of our surroundings and to ignore others is a central fact of perception. We come, in fact, to notice only a fraction of what is going on around us. Unless our attention is drawn to it, we do not notice the feel of our clothes on our skin, or the pressure of the ground under our feet, or the rims of our spectacles or the tips of our noses. It is not necessary for us to notice any of these things in the normal course of events. But we should be instantly aware if any of these sources of stimulation were removed, so that it is a *change* of stimulation rather than stimulation as such that we notice. An unchanging stimulus is quickly ignored; a process known as 'habituation'. This is an important factor in some forms of meditation. We also cease to pay attention to skilled performances such as walking, cycling or even driving a car, although while we are acquiring such skills they claim our closest attention. Even more automatic are skills like breathing and swallowing. This process of coming to behave automatically is known as 'automatization', and again a reversal of the process, that is, paying conscious attention to skilled actions, is also used in some forms of meditation.

What we notice and what we ignore will also depend on our pattern of interests: the townsman and countryman walking together down a country lane will notice quite different things, partly as a result of earlier learning and partly as a result of

16

differing interests. Psychologically speaking they will be walking down different lanes.

Apart from these factors of mood and interest and learning, what we attend to and what we ignore will largely depend on our motivation at the time. If I wish to walk down the pavement of a busy street, and I am in a hurry, I shall notice the people in my path, but I am less likely to notice the clouds in the sky, the chimneys on the roof tops, or the goods in the shop windows.

We always perceive more than our senses tell us

As well as being selective in what we perceive, we also add a great deal from past experience. We have to learn to associate experiences of different kinds. Thus when we say that ice looks cold or that food looks tasty, what we are doing is to say that on the basis of past experience, when an object has a certain appearance we know that when we touch it it will feel cold, or when we taste it, we shall like its taste. We learn to *see* roughness and smoothness, softness and hardness, although these experiences are inferences from quite other types of sensation. Again, to this extent, our perceptual worlds are of our own creation. This makes it possible for conjurors to create their illusions: they make us fill in according to our past experience, and to make assumptions about what we see for which we have no direct evidence. Thus we assume, when the conjuror stuffs a silk handkerchief into a box, that the sides are solid like other boxes we have experienced in the past, and do not suspect that he is stuffing the handkerchief into a hollow space in one of the solid-seeming sides. Thus when he shows us the inside of the box later, the handkerchief appears magically to have vanished.

It follows, then, that a vast amount of interpretation, evaluation, matching with memories of similar experiences

17

and so on, goes on all the time, so that as a result of past learning we add to the data our senses provide, from our storehouse of previous experiences. Thus as well as selection in perception, there is also addition and interpretation.

How we perceive others

When two people meet, they often react to one another, especially if they are strangers, in terms of the roles they are playing, rather than as two people acting in their own right, or as individuals 'doing their own thing'. If we see a postman coming to the front door with our letters, we perceive and react to him as a postman fulfilling a well-defined role. We say such things to him as are appropriate to say to a postman, and he is likely to react in a postmanlike way. We should not expect him to put his postbag down and begin to weed the garden, or to get a ladder and begin to clean the windows. These are actions expected of gardeners and window cleaners. However, in a village, we may know the postman in other roles; we may know his wife and family, his children may go to the same school as our own, we may meet him from time to time at the village pub or community centre. We shall almost certainly know his name. In towns there are too many people to make this possible or comfortable, so we protect ourselves by allotting roles to people, and reacting to them in a stereotyped way.

Role-playing has its social advantages. For instance, we are able to tell a doctor intimate details about ourselves, just because he is playing a doctor role. Indeed, many people prefer not to know their doctor socially, liking to maintain the role they have cast for him, uncomplicated by having to react to him differently on social occasions. Although role-playing helps to make certain situations easier to manage, it inevitably places people at a distance from each other, making it difficult

18

to break the barrier between them. A true meeting of persons must involve going behind the role, status or social class, and seeing the person in his own right. When we begin to love someone, we begin to feel that person is unique and incapable of being classified or allotted a role. Indeed, people quite understandably object to being classified in this way. William James put it well when he wrote:

> Probably a crab would be filled with a sense of personal outrage if it could hear us class it without ado or apology as a crustacean, and thus dispose of it. 'I am no such thing', it would say, 'I am *myself, myself* alone!'[10]

Quakers with their repudiation of titles, their insistence on treating people alike regardless of sex, status or position, have as much as any, attempted to meet people as people and not as players of roles. Their refusal, for example, to institute a central role of 'priest' may be a reflection of this in part, although the prime reason was more fundamental. Margaret Fell, the wife of George Fox, once sent a memorandum to Charles II 'from Margaret Fell to Charles Stuart'. Quakers appoint some of their number as 'Elders' and 'Overseers'. But these are temporary and functional roles, and are only conferred on certain named Friends to ensure that eldering and oversight shall be done. The appointment of a Friend as 'Clerk' of a business meeting applies to that particular meeting only when the Friend appointed has to introduce the business and record the minutes. He or she plays no special role in any other meeting.

When we are able to go behind the role or stereotype and meet and react to the person himself, we may experience what is described in the next chapter as being-cognition: seeing the person in and for himself and not in terms of our own needs and desires. But we may know very little about that person other than what we perceive at the time or on the basis of what little we have heard about him previously. There is a sort of instant intimacy about this way of reacting to people which is not the same as friendship. This is a later stage which develops over a period of time as we learn more about the person. We then accept and love him or her in spite of, and because of, all we have come to know about them.

How we perceive ourselves

I described in the first chapter how the developing individual has to learn to see himself as a unique and recognizable personality separate from his surroundings and from other people.

This awareness of a separate identity is probably achieved in stages. Adam Curle's book *Mystics and Militants*[11] has a chapter on 'Identity' in which he describes two such stages: the achievement of belonging-identity and the achievement of awareness-identity. Belonging-identity arises when we see ourselves as belonging to a well-defined group: class, culture or religious sect. An example might be when we perceive ourselves as middle-class English Quakers. Awareness-identity arises when we begin to be aware of our differences from others rather than our similarities. We then perceive our uniqueness or, as Adam Curle puts it, our 'complexity and diversity'.

This accords very well with what I have been saying about seeing others either as players of roles or as unique individuals. We can, likewise, see ourselves as role-players when we achieve belonging-identity, and as our unique selves when we achieve awareness-identity. Adam Curle's theory suggests that greater personal insight and self-knowledge lead to the strengthening of awareness-identity, and the weakening of belonging-identity; but he is also careful to point out that this should lead in turn, to a greater rather than a diminished awareness of others and their needs.

III

NEEDS AND BLINKERS

In this chapter, I shall give an account of human needs and how they may modify our perception of the world and of other people, and of how they may modify what we think about and even how we think. Such needs can and do act as blinkers constraining us to perceive and think in certain restricted ways.

Human needs and motives
Our perception and our thinking occur most often in accordance with our needs and intentions of the moment. In order to understand more clearly how this happens, I must now describe the human needs that are most likely to be concerned. A helpful account of human needs has been given by Abraham Maslow whose description of their role in perception is an important part of his theory. The following account is largely based on two of Maslow's books *Motivation and Personality*[12] and *Toward a Psychology of Being*.[13]

Physical needs. Why do men behave in the way they do? What makes them tick? At the primitive level a person behaves in certain ways, like any other animal, because he has some basic need to satisfy. If he is hungry he will seek food until that hunger is satisfied. When he becomes hungry once more, his behaviour will again be directed to seeking food. There are a number of needs at this level: air, food, water, rest, sleep, elimination of waste products, physical exercise, sensory stimulation, warmth and shelter. We have already seen, for example, how essential sensory stimulation is for the development of the body image and for the learning processes that lead to efficient perception. If any of these needs are denied to any great extent a man will take steps to meet them. If he fails to do so, he will fall ill and finally die of lack of air, hunger, thirst or exposure as the case may be. Although there are other needs of a psychological nature which I shall describe in the next section, these physical needs are prepotent and normally take precedence over any others. I say 'normally' because there are occasions when, for example, people go without food for psychopathological reasons as in *anorexia nervosa*, or for altruistic reasons when food is very short and they give their share away to others.

Psychological needs. Once the physical needs have been sufficiently met so as not to dominate man's behaviour, other needs become operative. These are the psychological needs such as the need to love and be loved, the need to be safe and secure from danger or the imminent threat of danger; and the need to be esteemed by others and to have a good or at least a tolerable opinion of oneself. People do not have to be taught to escape from situations they think are dangerous, or to seek to achieve loving relationships with other people. These things come naturally. Babies, if lovingly nursed, will grow to love their mothers and will express this love naturally. They will also seek to escape from things which frighten them, and will show every sign of distress in situations they think will harm them.

The esteem needs are less obvious and are less generally accepted as being in the same category. The distress caused by feelings of inferiority is obvious enough. We have all probably suffered from this at times, and we all know people whose main motivation in life seems to be to prove that they are worthy of our good opinion, and parade their achievements for general approval. Nevertheless, the idea that esteem is a basic human need runs counter to much of our secular and religious teaching. We are told that we must not show off, that pride comes before a fall, that modesty is a virtue. Yet unless we have a good opinion of ourselves, we shall not feel worthy of other people's love, and consequently will find it hard to seek and receive the love of others. To some extent, of course, this is a two-way process: if we realize that people *do* seem to love us, then we tend to assume that we cannot be so bad after all, that there must be something loveable about us. Some religious teaching which emphasizes our sinfulness seems to provide a positive hindrance to the achievement of self-esteem. In a little pamphlet called *Interpretation of Quakerism.* Rufus Jones writes that 'Quakerism proposes to drop overboard the whole heavy load of theological notions, including the depravity of man'.[14] Friends have never been much concerned with the essential sinfulness of man. George Fox's call from Launceston prison was to '. . . walk cheerfully over the world, answering that of God in everyone'.[15]

If these psychological needs are not met, a person may become neurotic or chronically anxious, in the same way that he would become physically ill or under par if his physical needs were not met. The physical and psychological needs have been called the *deficiency needs* since they arise when there is some deficiency in the environment which prevents the individual from satisfying his basic physical or psychological requirements.

Growth motives. Once the physical and psychological needs have been met, why does a man not sit down and twiddle his thumbs? Or go to sleep? What happens is that another set of motives now make their appearance. These are the ones that lead to further growth and development of the personality, and are thus known as the *growth motives*. If for some reason they remain inoperative or frustrated or unsatisfied, the individual does not become physically ill or neurotic, but is unlikely to achieve further development of the personality. These growth motives are curiosity, aesthetic appreciation, and what Maslow calls 'self-actualization'. This latter is the drive which many people have to develop their talents, to actualize their potential, to make the most of themselves. It is these motives that drive the adequately fed, secure, loved and esteemed scientist to seek fresh discoveries and new knowledge, that drive the artist to seek aesthetic experience and creative work, that drive many of us to develop our potential as far as circumstances will allow. The growth motives of curiosity and aesthetic experience are fairly obvious and probably need no more discussion. Self-actualization besides being an awkward and somewhat clumsy term, is also liable to be misunderstood, and to be associated with a selfish personal ambition. In fact it means becoming truly ourselves, realizing or making real all that is in us to be. Since man is a social animal, nurtured and trained in a social context, he cannot be himself by himself. His further development, his self-actualization, has to be achieved, indeed can only be achieved, in harmony with his social environment and with the help and cooperation of other people.

The hierarchy of motives. As I have already said, the physical needs are prepotent and take precedence over the others. This means that if a man is desperately hungry he may behave in such a way to obtain food as to place him in danger or to earn him the disesteem or hatred of his fellows. This, of course, is not invariably so. Some heroic characters like Gandhi will deliberately starve in prison in order to uphold an ideal more important than life itself. Some people who have been imprisoned for pursuing some political or other cause identified with a close-knit minority group, may refuse food in order to keep the esteem of that group whose good opinion is more valuable to them than anything else.

In the same way, higher up the scale as it were, a person may have his basic physical needs met, he may be admirably fed, sheltered, clothed and so on, but he may still feel unloved, disesteemed and insecure. Children in pre-war orphanages and institutions were often in just this position. In these circumstances, a person may be unaware of any motives of curiosity or aesthetic appreciation just because he is too busy seeking to love or to be loved, or to earn the good opinion of others. We are not likely to take time off to enjoy the sunset if we are miserable and frightened. Once again this general principle will be subject to other factors. One, of course, is the severity of the deprivation concerned. We might go to a concert directly after work and forgo our supper to do so, but we might feel less inclined to do this if we had had no food at all during the day, even if we had not been to a concert for years.

Howard Collier in his pamphlet *The Quaker Meeting*[16] suggests that the effect of hunger, insecurity and so on, is to make us egocentric and unable to turn our attention away from our personal affairs.

> A hungry man cannot perform Thy service.
> I beg for a bed with four legs on it:
> I beg for a quilt to cover me;
> And then, Thy servant, will devotedly worship Thee.

He goes on to write:

> It is true that fasting will help the *well-fed* to meditate, but chronic starvation, or an over-riding sense of fear or of injustice, or hatred, guilt or shame serve only to

25

3

concentrate our attention upon the self and to arrest self-detachment.

Deficiency-cognition and being-cognition

It has been important to explain this theory about human needs and their hierarchical arrangement, since this has a direct bearing on the way we experience people and things. We can see them either in terms of our own needs and as potential satisfiers of those needs; or we can see them in quite a different way, that is in and for themselves, undistorted by any self-centred need or desire. It is clear that the first kind of cognition, seeing people in terms of our own needs, is likely to occur when we are subject to the deficiency needs already described. The second kind of cognition, unaffected by personal need, is more likely to occur when we are subject to the growth motives already described. The first kind of cognition Maslow called *deficiency-cognition* or D-cognition, associated with deficiency needs; and the second kind of cognition he called *being-cognition* or B-cognition, associated with growth motives. It might help to list the important attributes of each kind of cognition.

D-cognition	*B-cognition*
Active	Passive
Interfering	Non-interfering, accepting, detached
Selective	Non-selective
Desiring	Loving
Subjective, self-centred	Objective, selfless
Distorted, partial	Undistorted, full
Based on deficiency needs	Based on growth motives

26

It is important to emphasize that there is no suggestion that one kind of cognition is 'better' or 'more valuable' than the other, although one will certainly be more appropriate than the other in any given circumstance. Our prevailing pattern of needs of the moment will predispose us to one or other kind of cognition. It is however probably true that most of us find we are using D-cognition most of the time, and B-cognition only rarely, just because we are inevitably immersed in the scurry and turmoil of daily living and coping, and have little time to 'stand and stare'.

There is a splendid example of the contrast between deficiency-cognition and being-cognition in Helen Waddell's book *The Desert Fathers*, where she records a meeting of bishops addressed by Bishop Nonnus in the open air outside the doors of the Basilica at Antioch:

And as we sat, certain of the bishops besought my master Nonnus that they might have some instruction from his lips: and straightway the good bishop began to speak to the weal and health of all that heard him. And as we sat marvelling at the holy learning of him, lo! on a sudden she that was first of the actresses of Antioch passed by: first of the dancers was she, and riding on an ass: and with all fantastic graces did she ride, so decked that naught could be seen upon her but gold and pearls and precious stones: the very nakedness of her feet was hidden under gold and pearls; and with her was a splendid train of young men and maidens clad in robes of price, with torques of gold about their necks. Some went before and some came after her: but of the beauty and the loveliness of her there could be no wearying for a world of men. Passing through our midst, she filled the air with the fragrance of musk and of all scents that are sweetest. And when the bishops saw her so shamelessly ride by, bare of head and shoulder

27

and limb, in pomp so splendid, and not so much as a veil upon her head or about her shoulders, they groaned, and in silence turned away their heads as from great and grievous sin. But the most blessed Nonnus did long and most intently regard her: and after she had passed by still he gazed and still his eyes went after her. Then, turning his head, he looked upon the bishops sitting round him. 'Did not', said he, 'the sight of her great beauty delight you?'[17]

Here was a man able to see physical beauty with true B-cognition, without desire, in the full, detached, non-interfering way so characteristic of this kind of perception.

The innocent eye

There is an innocence of vision about B-cognition, when all that one sees is new and fresh and perceived as if for the first time. Aldous Huxley in a passage quoted in the next chapter writes of seeing some flowers as Adam might have seen them on the first morning of creation. Not surprisingly B-cognition experiences are frequently recorded by people as having been experienced in childhood. This may well be because to the inexperienced child, much that he sees is so strange and new, that it does not have any need-fulfilling properties for him. Just because he does not know enough about the world, he does not know how he can use it and bend it to his purposes. He is therefore more free to see it in a detached way, as Adam perceived Eden on the morning of creation, pristine, dewy, fresh, not so much at the dawn of a new day, but at the start of the first day of all. One such childhood experience is described by Roger Bannister in his book *First Four Minutes*:[18]

I remember a moment when I stood barefoot on firm dry sand by the sea. The air had a special quality as if it had a life of its own. The sound of breakers on the shore shut out all others. I looked up at the clouds, like great white-sailed galleons, chasing proudly inland. I looked down at the regular ripples on the sand, and could not absorb so much beauty. I was taken aback—each of the myriad particles of sand was perfect in its way . . . there was nothing to detract from all this beauty.

Arthur Koestler suggests that innocence of perception, seeing things in a fresh new light, free from prejudices and preconceptions, lies at the heart of creative experience.

Every creative act—in science, art, or religion—involves a regression to a more primitive level, a new innocence of perception liberated from the cataract of accepted beliefs.[19]

The playfulness of creative thinking, often involving ideas which are downright funny and amusing, seems directly associated with innocence of perception, with its childish-seeming nature. We play about with ideas as with toys. We re-arrange them, toss them back and forth, and in the process we may hit upon something quite new, original and fruitful. Einstein's famous idea 'What would happen if I rode on a beam of light?' led to his Special Theory of Relativity. A number of writers have examined this kind of thinking. Edward de Bono[20] calls it 'lateral thinking'. Liam Hudson[21] calls it 'divergent thinking'. These in turn seem to be related to what is known as non-linear consciousness which I shall now describe.

Linear and non-linear consciousness

When we have to think out the solution to a problem, we have been taught to do so logically, step by step. If A is so, then it must follow that B is the case. If B, then C follows logically, and so on. This is deductive thinking in which conclusions are deduced from what has gone before. We have been trained to be conscious of events in much the same way. We become aware of things happening in sequence, one after another, one event causing the next.

Robert Ornstein has written an important book *The Psychology of Consciousness* in which he suggests that our thinking about, and interpretation of, events can be non-linear, so that they form a complex pattern, as happening in space rather than in time, as being simultaneous rather than sequential, uncaused rather than caused. He gives a striking example:

> That man is being taken to be hanged. Is that because someone gave him a silver piece and enabled him to buy the knife with which he committed the murder; or because someone saw him do it; or because nobody stopped him?[22]

This non-linear kind of thinking sometimes leads to the solution of a problem which is seen suddenly as a new pattern, configuration or gestalt. The playing about with ideas, described in the last section, may also lead to unexpected solutions to problems, just because new patterns can emerge by such means.

Up to this point, this essay has tried to follow the logical argument, the step by step building up of a point of view. From now onwards, I shall need to be non-linear in approach, throwing up various related ideas which may seem repetitive, overlapping, even contradictory. But they all attempt to approach the subject matter from different angles, in the hope that a general pattern may emerge. This is rather like studying a building by looking at various photographs taken from different viewpoints. They are repetitive, and overlapping, and sometimes apparently inconsistent, but they do in the end give a very good idea of what the building is like.

There is nothing new or strange about non-linear consciousness. We all experience it in dreams and fantasies, and it is deliberately cultivated in meditation and in many different traditional exercises designed to achieve religious or mystical experience.

Both being-cognition and non-linear thinking seem to be closely related to peak-experiences which I describe in the next chapter.

IV

THE DRIFT OF PINIONS

Not where the wheeling systems darken,
And our benumbed conceiving soars!—
The drift of pinions, would we hearken,
Beats at our own clay-shuttered doors.

—*The Kingdom of God* by Francis Thompson

Intimations of immortality

All down the ages men have asserted that there is more to
experience than an awareness of the external environment, or
of the internal world of thoughts, memories, dreams, emotions
and desires. They have asserted that there is another dimension
which somehow gives a hint of another aspect of the world
which, although usually hidden, seems infinitely more true and
beautiful than the world as experienced every day. This hint
comes not only from their perception of the world around
them, but also from awareness of their inner experiences, giving
an added dimension to each. We have seen that psychologists
have also presented evidence of an added dimension to outward
perception in being-cognition, and an added dimension to
inner experiences in non-linear thinking.

This added dimension has been variously interpreted as
being intimations of a spiritual world, a glimpse of heaven, or as
a manifestation of the presence of God. Some writers, like
Gerald Heard,[23] have suggested that this other world, this

added dimension, can only be experienced after a long and arduous spiritual training, that it is vouchsafed only to the fortunate and chosen few, the spiritual athletes, to those perhaps with a special gift or vocation to survive the rigours involved in its attainment. The ascetic tradition, especially favoured in the first century of the Christian Church and by some eastern religions, seems also to take this view.

Others seem to have had rather different experiences. Conspicuous among these are Francis Thompson and Hans Denck. Take for example Thompson's *Hound of Heaven*:

> I fled Him, down the nights and down the days;
> I fled Him, down the arches of the years,
> I fled Him, down the labyrinthine ways
> Of my own mind.[24]

Here the experience is in no way an arduous search for God, but rather of God's impetuous search for man. Hans Denck puts it differently, but the message is the same:

> Oh, my God, how does it happen in this poor old world, that Thou art so great and yet nobody finds Thee, that Thou callest so loudly and nobody hears Thee, that Thou art so near and nobody feels Thee, that Thou givest Thyself to everybody and nobody knows Thy name! Men flee from Thee and say they cannot find Thee; they turn their backs and say they cannot see Thee; they stop their ears and say they cannot hear Thee![25]

Naming the experience

Many people testify that from time to time they have an experience which seems to them to have a transcendent quality, an out of time or out of space dimension which sets it apart from everyday experience. As Arnold Toynbee put it, 'moments as memorable as they are rare in which temporal and spatial barriers fall and psychic distance is annihilated'.[26] A workable definition of these special experiences seems impossible—many writers have attempted it and failed. To be able to make such a definition would imply that all the experiences as reported had a common quality or qualities which could be clearly expressed in words. But by their very nature they are highly subjective and personal, notoriously difficult to pin down in intelligible verbal description. Pascal, usually so exact and skilful with words, could only describe one such experience with a single word, 'Fire!' This verbal difficulty will become evident later in this chapter where people's attempts to describe the indescribable are recorded. However, even when some record has been achieved, there are other difficulties, as Ninian Smart points out:

> There is a special difficulty, however, in undertaking a description of a religious experience . . . the experience occurred in the context of the existing religions which already had a doctrinal dimension . . . it is not easy to know about a given report which of the elements in it are based, so to say, purely on the experience itself, and which are due to doctrinal and mythological interpretation . . . experience and doctrinal interpretation have a dialectical relationship. The latter colours the former, but the former also shapes the latter.[27]

Marghanita Laski calls these experiences 'transcendent ecstasies',[28] Adam Curle writes of 'supraliminal awareness',[29] and Maslow refers to 'peak-experiences'.[30] The term 'timeless moments' might have been appropriate since the out of time dimension seems often to be the crucial one. However, I decided not to use this term since many of the descriptions which people have recorded do not mention timelessness as an important or essential characteristic. Consequently I shall use Maslow's term 'peak-experience' as it now appears widely in the literature. It has certain advantages, in that it suggests that the phenomenon concerned occurs only rarely and that it is highly valued. Moreover the term 'peak' carries the further important implication that these experiences are not wholly different from other more mundane experiences, but rather intensified examples of everyday events, just as a peak although rare, is still part of the landscape marked out for its height. The difference is one of degree rather than of kind. This idea is at variance with some of the descriptions of peak-experiences which seem to emphasize their 'wholly other' quality. However, the weight of evidence seems to suggest that *peak-experiences are rare and intense examples of being-cognition or non-linear consciousness.*

Triggers

The range of experiences recorded is immense, their nature clearly depending both on the cultural training of the experiencer and on the circumstances in which the experience occurred. Their intensity and duration vary, although the experience is typically very brief and often described as lasting only a moment. They are usually recognized at the time as having a special quality, although they are sometimes only recognized for what they are in retrospect. They are, most commonly, 'triggered', to use Marghanita Laski's useful term[31] by scenes of natural beauty, religious rituals and practices both by individuals on their own and in groups, aesthetic perception and creative achievement, scientific discovery and intellectual insight, sexual experience, childbirth, athletic achievement, and in moments of personal crisis especially when insight is achieved. Social interaction with one or several other people, especially when sharing a common purpose, is also a well known trigger. Some drugs apparently produce experiences which seem very like peak-experiences, although there are important differences which I shall mention later.

Examples of peak-experiences

Peak-experiences vary from the apparently trivial and banal, to the shattering experience of a St Paul which may totally change the direction of the individual's later life. I shall now consider a number of reports of these experiences, selected to show their range and diversity, and the probable triggers which preceded them, or the context in which they occurred. There are many famous collections of such experiences, but I must pay particular tribute to Marghanita Laski's book *Ecstasy*[32] from which I have been able to take some of my examples, and which has stimulated me to think afresh about the many problems involved in a study of this kind.

Arising from scenes of natural beauty. My first two examples appear to have been triggered by scenes of natural beauty. These form one of the most common triggers in Laski's collection. Richard Jefferies in *The Story of my Heart* records this experience:

> I looked at the hills, at the dewy grass, and then up through the elm branches to the sky. In a moment all that was behind me, the house, the people, the sounds, seemed to disappear, and leave me alone. Involuntarily I drew a long breath, then I breathed slowly. My thought, or inner consciousness, went up through the illumined sky, and I was lost in a moment of exaltation. This only lasted a very short time, perhaps only part of a second, and while it lasted there was no formulated wish. I was absorbed; I drank the beauty of the morning; I was exalted.[33]

Howard Collier in his pamphlet *The Quaker Meeting*, recounts a less intense experience, but nevertheless one that has many typical features:

> About two years ago on an April morning, I felt ill at ease and unhappy. Life was difficult and the burden of the war

weighed upon me. I climbed the steep path at the entrance of one of our public parks and stood beneath some cherry trees that fringe the crest of the bank. A fresh wind blew dark clouds across the green-blue sky. The white blossom shone and glistened in the sunlight. As I stood relaxed and still, I had the illusion that I was enveloped in light. I had the feeling that the light and I were one. Time and space slipped from me. All awareness of details vanished. A sense of unity with the world entered into me. I was tranquillized and steaded by the beauty, the stability of Nature. I do not suppose that I learnt anything that was new to me during the experience. But I believe I was taught something and that something happened in me. I returned to my work tranquil, and strengthened in faith and hope by my experience.[34]

Religious experiences. Peak-experiences occurring in a religious context, or considered to be of a religious nature, are widely reported. Indeed, many of the famous collections contain records of this nature almost exclusively. I shall only quote one which shall stand as typical of its kind. Many of them, like the one quoted below, report a feeling of the presence of God. It is taken from one of the most famous of all religious collections, *The Varieties of Religious Experience* by William James:

There was not a mere consciousness of something there, but fused in the central happiness of it, a startling awareness of some ineffable good. Not vague either, not like the emotional effect of some poem, or scene, or blossom, or music, but the sure knowledge of the close presence of a sort of mighty person, and after it went, the memory persisted as the one perception of reality. Everything else might be a dream, but not that.[35]

This is a valuable example, since the writer carefully distinguishes the experience from the 'emotional effect' of aesthetic experience. The defining characteristics of being-cognition and peak-experiences which make them so much more than 'emotional effect' are set out in the next chapter.

Arising from scientific discovery. C. P. Snow in his book *The Search*, describes a peak-experience associated with scientific discovery:

> Then I was carried beyond pleasure. I have tried to show something of the high moments that science gave to me . . . But this was different from any of them, different altogether, different in kind. It was further from myself. My own triumph and delight and success were there, but they seemed insignificant beside this tranquil ecstasy. It was as though I had looked for a truth outside myself, and finding it had become for a moment part of the truth I sought; as though the world, the atoms and the stars, were wonderfully clear and close to me, and I to them, so that we were part of a lucidity more tremendous than any mystery.[36]

Arising from uneasiness, distress and personal crisis. Howard Collier in the report quoted above writes of his feeling ill at ease and unhappy before he had his peak-experience. Often this unhappiness or even despair, seems to play a part in triggering a peak-experience especially if it involves some personal crisis. The following example, well known to Quakers, concerns John Wilhelm Rowntree as a young man:

> Just as he was entering young manhood and was beginning to feel the dawning sense of a great mission before him, he discovered that he was slowly losing his sight. He was

told that before middle life he would become totally blind. Dazed and overwhelmed he staggered from the doctor's office to the street and stood there in silence. Suddenly he felt the love of God wrap him about as though a visible presence enfolded him, and a joy filled him, such as he had never known before.[37]

Drug-induced experiences. It has long been known that some drugs cause experiences in those who take them which have some features similar to peak-experiences, although others are quite untypical. For example drug experiences are not momentary and out of time, in the way that spontaneous peak-experiences usually are. They do however seem to be invested with great meaning and significance. Such experiences are by no means the invariable result of taking the so-called psychedelic drugs. Sometimes they are horrifying, unedifying, meaningless and disintegrating in nature. It seems to depend in some measure on the personality and expectations of the drug taker. The person supervising 'the trip' apparently can, to some extent, modify by suggestion the nature of the experience. Marghanita Laski quotes an interesting account of what seemed to be a peak experience occurring during anaesthesia with nitrous oxide.

> Whilst under the anaesthetic for a short operation, I had a complete revelation about the ultimate truth of everything. I understood the 'entire works'. It was a tremendous illumination. I was filled with unspeakable joy. . . . When I came round I told the doctor I understand the meaning of everything. He . . . said, 'Well, what is it?' and I faltered out, 'Well, it's a sort of green light.'[38]

This example nicely illustrates the great difficulty that people have in describing such experiences. It takes an Aldous Huxley to do verbal justice to them. Here is his description of what it

40

is like to see the world under mescalin intoxication. It is taken from his essay *The Doors of Perception*:

> The vase contained only three flowers. . . . I had been struck by the lively dissonance of its colours. But that was no longer the point. I was not looking now at an unusual flower arrangement. I was seeing what Adam had seen on the morning of his creation—the miracle, moment by moment, of naked existence. . . . The books, for example, . . . they glowed . . . with brighter colours, a profounder significance . . . so intense, so intrinsically meaningful that they seemed to be on the point of leaving the shelves to thrust themselves more insistently on my attention.[39]

This so-called 'Adamic experience' is often a feature of being-cognition. Of interest too, in this description, is that his concentrated attention to what he is experiencing seems to stem from the objects themselves which 'thrust themselves more insistently' on his attention. He does not have to make any determined effort to pay attention to his surroundings, they are intrinsically so interesting that no effort is needed on his part, any more than the lover has to try hard to pay attention to his beloved.

Desolation experiences. Less frequently people have reported experiences of desolation rather than of ecstasy, which have nevertheless seemed to them to be valuable and rewarding, and seem also to have many of the features of peak-experiences. Laski quotes from Thomas Traherne who had an experience at the age of four which he reports in later life:

> In a lowering and sad evening, being alone in the field, when all things were dead and quiet, a certain want and horror fell upon me, beyond imagination. The unprofitableness and silence of the place dissatisfied me: its

41

wideness terrified me: from the utmost ends of the earth fears surrounded me. . . . I was a weak and little child, and had forgotten there was a man alive in the earth. Yet something also of hope and expectation comforted me from every border. This taught me that I was concerned in all the world.[40]

Bridging the gap

By definition peak-experiences are rare. In order to highlight their distinctive features I have selected some of the more remarkable examples. The great majority of being-cognition experiences are set in a lower key, less intense, but nevertheless no different in kind from peak-experiences, which include the beatific vision of the saint, the rapture of the mystic, the creative vision of the artist or the scientific insight of an Einstein. They all seem to bridge the gap between the world of becoming, set in the inexorable progress of time with events causing and being caused, viewed through the distorting spectacles of our desire; and the world of being, timeless, patterned, uncaused, viewed in all its meaning and significance with our uncritical and loving acceptance.

Most people have had moments of joy or rapture, often with the characteristic timeless quality, intense enough to be memorable and thought provoking. These experiences may come when one falls in love, or has a child on one's lap or when one is confronted with the unexpected kindness of a stranger. These moments happen, of course, in private prayer and communal worship. As Thomas Kelly puts it:

> The gathered meeting I take to be of the same kind, still milder and more diffused, yet really of a piece with all mystical experience. For mystical times are capable of all gradings and shadings, from sublime heights to very mild moments of lift and very faint glimpses of glory.[41]

42

These are all within range of most people's experience. Maslow, indeed, considers that it is exceptional for a person to be able truthfully to claim that he has never had an experience of this kind. Since all experiences are individual and cannot be shared, it is inevitable that all the descriptions are related as William James puts it 'to man in his solitude'.[42] Although experiences within the group such as in meeting for worship, may lead to non-linear thinking or being-cognition and occasionally to a peak-experience, the phenomenon itself from its very nature remains personal, individual, private and unshared.

V

STANDING STILL IN THE LIGHT

> And stand still in the Light, and submit
> to it, and the other will be hushed and
> gone; and then content comes.
> —George Fox, 1652

From the very large number of accounts of being-cognition and peak-experience which are now available in the literature, it seems clear that their nature varies according to the particular trigger that gave rise to them, to the personality of the experiencer, his past experiences, present pattern of needs and expectations, and particularly to the cultural *milieu* in which he has been nurtured.

For all the variations so caused, peak-experiences seem to be highly valued, rewarding, usually pleasant or even ecstatic. They involve a marked concentration of attention, are typically brief in duration and are experienced as timeless or out of time. They often include a profound sense of understanding of the meaning of life, or as psychologists might put it, a completion of the pattern or gestalt. Perhaps most consistently of all, the experiencer loses his self-awareness in his total absorption in the experience so that he feels he has become part of what he perceives. I shall consider each of these features in turn.

Concentrated attention
The ability to select some feature of the environment and to pay close attention to it, is an important factor in being-cog-

45

nition. It involves however, more than close attention. The perceiver, as he attends to something in this way, finds that he is accepting it in and for itself. He does not classify or judge or evaluate it or compare it with anything else. He sees someone as a person in his or her own right, unique and unclassifiable. He sees a crab as *that* crab and not as a crustacean. In attending to the person or object, he wants nothing from it, does not want to alter or change it in any way, he accepts it for what it is. Richard Jefferies in the passage quoted earlier wrote of having 'no formulated wish'.

Evelyn Underhill has a remarkable passage in her book *Mysticism*, in which she describes the results of attending to something in this concentrated way:

All that is asked is that we shall look for a little time, in a special and undivided manner, at some simple, concrete and external thing. This object of our contemplation may be almost anything we please: a picture, a statue, a tree, a distant hillside, a growing plant, running water, little living things. . . . Look, then, at this thing which you have chosen. Wilfully yet tranquilly refuse the messages which countless other aspects of the world are sending; and so concentrate your whole attention on this one act of loving sight that all other objects are excluded from the conscious field. Do not think, but as it were pour out your personality towards it: let your soul be in your eyes. Almost at once, this new method of perception will reveal unexpected qualities in the external world. First, you will perceive about you a strange and deepening quietness: a slowing down of our feverish mental time. Next, you will become aware of a heightened significance, an intensified existence in the thing at which you look. As you, with all your consciousness, lean out towards it, an answering current will meet yours. It seems as though the barrier

46

between its life and your own, between subject and object, had melted away. You are merged with it, in an act of true communion: and you *know* the secret of its being deeply and unforgettably, yet in a way which you can never hope to express. Seen thus, a thistle has celestial qualities: a speckled hen a touch of the sublime.[43]

This description contains all the features characteristic of being-cognition, and was of course written half a century before Maslow described being-cognition in modern terms. He too, writes of the 'tremendous concentration of a kind which does not usually occur' when we are experiencing this kind of perception.

Paying concentrated attention to something may, especially in the early stages, involve a great deal of hard work. But this is because we are still fighting against distraction. Evelyn Underhill warns against making too much of a fight of it. 'Wilfully yet tranquilly refuse the messages which countless other aspects of the world are sending' is her advice. But if we find the object of our attention sufficiently attractive, no conscious effort to attend is required on our part. The lover does not have to strive to attend to his beloved because he finds that other things do not distract him. He has eyes for no one else. Thus if we surrender to our experience we become absorbed, as Richard Jeffries recorded, until finally we are claimed by it and become part of that which we experience.

The timeless moment
Evelyn Underhill wrote of 'a slowing down of our feverish mental time'. Howard Collier recorded that 'time and space slipped from me'. These references to a change in the experience of time occur again and again in descriptions of being-cognition and peak-experience. This is almost certainly closely associated with the concentrated attention so characteristic of being-

47

cognition. When we concentrate hard on some external source of stimulation, time seems to pass more slowly, or a given length of time seems to have lasted longer than expected. Robert Ornstein, viewing the problem from the point of view of a physiological psychologist, states that 'an increase of vigilance (i.e. attention) should result in a greater amount of awareness of input and consequently in a lengthening of duration experience.'[44] Laski has several references to this experience in her collection of ecstasy reports:

> timeless bliss, sensation of timelessness, a complete absence of a sense of time and place, a complete suspension of time, standstill feeling, etc., etc.[45]

Richard Jefferies recorded that his experience 'lasted for a very short time, perhaps only part of a second' and yet it was a highly meaningful experience. The timelessness of these experiences is, of course, something that is sought after by meditation techniques.

Poetic references to the timeless moment are numerous. T. S. Eliot's poem *Burnt Norton* contains a celebrated example:

> At the still point of the turning world. Neither
> flesh nor fleshless;
> Neither from nor towards; at the still point, there
> the dance is,
> But neither arrest nor movement.[46]

Meaning, significance, understanding

Evelyn Underhill wrote of 'heightened significance'. Howard Collier recorded that 'a sense of the unity of the world entered into me'. C. P. Snow wrote of 'a lucidity more tremendous than any mystery'. The girl coming round from the anaesthetic claimed that she had had a revelation of the ultimate truth of everything, and that she understood the 'entire works'. Aldous

Huxley recorded his sense of a profounder significance, that things were so intrinsically meaningful.

Marghanita Laski's collection abounds with similar descriptions:

> suddenly clicked—perception of a pattern, sensation of absolute oneness, the whole world falls into place—matches—fits, all creation came into harmony, sense of something being perfected, everything is right and all the world makes sense, etc., etc.[47]

This impressive array of evidence fits in very well with Ornstein's account of the patterned thinking of non-linear consciousness. This is what psychologists call 'closure': the sudden perception of a meaningful pattern or gestalt in what previously appeared to be a meaningless jumble of sensations or ideas. Such closure is usually highly satisfying to the person who experiences it, and the reassurance it gives is an important feature of being-cognition.

Sense of being part of a larger whole

Once again we can begin with a quotation from Evelyn Underhill. In the passage already referred to several times, she records:

> It seems as though the barrier between its life and your own, between subject and object, has melted away. You are merged with it in an act of true communion.[48]

This is a characteristic feature of being-cognition and may well stem from the concentrated attention involved and the perception of an overall pattern and wholeness. This came out clearly in the passage from C. P. Snow, 'I had looked for a truth outside myself, and finding it had become for a moment part of the truth I sought.' Howard Collier wrote, 'I had a feeling that the light and I were one.' Thomas Traherne realized that he 'was concerned in all the world'. Once again Marghanita Laski has many examples:

> the hard lines of one's individuality are gone, a state of not being oneself, a feeling of identification with the whole sensible universe, a loss of the sense of being yourself, a feeling of oneness with the totality of nature, etc., etc.[49]

One of Maslow's criteria for being-cognition is that it is unmotivated and impersonal. In any case, any great concentration of attention would be expected to lead to a loss of awareness of self since we cannot pay attention to ourselves when we are concentrating hard on something else. However this is not the same as the loss of self. Horace Pointing in an article in *The Friend* puts this clearly:

> What is meant by saying that all of the self has to go before we can really know God? The assertion seems to me to be open to some misunderstanding. Self-surrender is not an achievement in piety. The surrender is of the *isolated* self. What is lost is the isolation, not the self; and what endures is the consciousness of that relationship between our own essential being and God.[50]

Beyond good and evil

In the chapter on perception I explained that it was change in stimulation rather than stimulation as such that gave rise to meaningful perception. This change can, of course, be spatial as well as temporal. We can only make sense of what we see because there are spatial and temporal discontinuities. Things stop and start, move about, have edges, are shaded, are variously coloured and so on. Without these changes in space and time we should not be aware of movement, nor shape nor depth, nor of figures standing out against backgrounds. Moreover we should soon become incapable of paying attention to such a homogeneous and unchanging environment.

The idea of the reconciliation of opposites follows directly from this simple and basic fact of perception. To become aware of a hill we must also be aware of the plain. If we stood in the middle of an extensive moor all of which is equally high, we should not see it as hilly. At a more abstract level, we cannot be aware of beauty unless we can compare it with ugliness, kindness unless we know cruelty, truth unless we know the nature of falsehood, good unless evil also exists. The awareness of one necessitates the existence of the other.

Awareness of the world of being involves awareness of both good and evil within the same overall pattern, the one implying the other. Hermann Hesse in his novel *Narziss and Goldmund* describes this awareness of the good and the bad, the desirable and the undesirable, and the essential reconciliation between them. The wood carver Goldmund describes his vision of the world of being in the following terms:

> The thing I love and hanker for is mysterious. I am on its track. I have seen it in flashes several times and, as a carver, when I can do so, I mean to shape it till it reveals itself. Its form shall be the form of the mother of all things. Her beauty, unlike that of other figures, shall not consist in any particular, no special roundness or slenderness, plainness or decorated form, winsomeness or strength, but in this—that in her the furthest opposites shall be reconciled, living together in my work: birth and death, pleasure and pain, life and destruction; all which, outside her, could never make peace in the world.[51]

Peggy Makins, in a radio broadcast, described a peak-experience in which the reconciliation of good and evil seemed an important feature.

> I was aware of being lifted up on a tide of love, warm, tingling, buoyant; love was all around me, I breathed it, felt it animate me. In that moment I loved everything,

everybody, evil and dirt were transfigured into the necessities they are. For three weeks after that holy day I felt I walked with my feet inches above the ground, my mind working furiously on the new notion of evil as the reverse of the coin of good, one inseparable from the other.[52]

William James has an interesting comment on his own experiences under the influence of nitrous oxide:

Looking back on my own experiences they all converge towards a kind of insight to which I cannot help ascribing some metaphysical significance. The keynote of it is invariably a reconciliation. It is as if the opposites of the world, whose contradictoriness and conflict make all our difficulties and troubles, were melted into unity.[53]

Peak-experiences and being-cognition are universally considered to be desirable and rewarding, although for the reasons stated above they may involve elements of evil, ugliness, pain and suffering. Maslow discusses this point as follows:

The world is accepted. People will say that then they understand it. Most important of all for comparison with religious thinking is that somehow they become reconciled to evil. Evil itself is accepted and understood and seen in its proper place in the whole, as belonging there, as unavoidable, as necessary, and, therefore, as proper. . . . It is as if the peak-experience reconciled people to the presence of evil in the world.[54]

Non-linear consciousness, with its awareness of pattern rather than of cause and effect, leads people to regard good and evil as both parts of the pattern and both necessary to it. Indeed, in the context of non-linear consciousness, they may not appear as good or evil at all, since these terms are often used subjectively without any absolute meaning. Thus dust may be seen as matter in the wrong place, weeds as plants where they are not wanted, visual ugliness as misplaced shape and colour, and so on. It is this way of perceiving the world that makes sense of Lady Julian's phrase 'all manner of thing shall be well', which, seen in the context of the world of becoming, might sound like a facile optimism bearing little relation to things as they really seem to be.

Meditation

Before discussing the relation between being-cognition, non-linear consciousness and Quaker worship, I must first say something about meditation.

Naranjo and Ornstein in a review of the wide variety of meditation techniques, came to the conclusion that meditation always involves a 'dwelling upon something' and that the practice of meditation generally involves an effort 'to set our attention upon a single object, sensation, utterance, issue, mental state or activity'.[55]

Thus from the outset we can see a feature common to both meditation and being-cognition, namely concentrated attention. Meditation techniques seem to be concerned with paying concentrated attention either to some feature of the external environment, or to internal experiences. These techniques seem to be designed to modify a person's mental state so that he or she comes to experience the external environment or his or her internal world of thoughts and images, in a different and fruitful way. Two contrasting techniques aim either at *opening up* a person's awareness of his surroundings or at *turning off* such awareness so that he may the more easily concentrate on his inner experiences.

Opening up technique. This technique was beautifully described by Evelyn Underhill in the passage quoted earlier in which the speckled hen achieved a touch of the sublime. This seems to lead directly to being-cognition, when the object,

53

person or scene is experienced in all its richness and splendour, meaning and significance. The perceiver's love for the object is aroused and his unity with it deeply felt. In a real sense the perceiver surrenders to the experience unconditionally and is content to be exposed to all it can do to and for him. I described in an earlier chapter how we are normally aware of only a fraction of the stimulation that comes our way. Some of the filtering is of course physiological: we are not physically capable of becoming aware of certain energy sources. But some of the filtering is psychological: we do not notice things because we do not need to or want to. I also pointed out that we tend not to notice an unchanging stimulus when we become habituated to it. Similarly, we come to perform certain actions automatically, such as breathing, swallowing, walking and so on. Robert Ornstein suggests that certain techniques of meditation attempt to dehabituate our awareness and deautomatize our actions.[56] We thus deliberately pay attention to stimuli we should normally not notice, as Evelyn Underhill suggests, and pay close attention to automatic actions like breathing, swallowing, and so on. In this way we widen our range of awareness, and experience events perhaps less distorted by our pattern of needs or current motivations, or by our stereotyped habits. Aldous Huxley suggests that this technique of meditation may lead to 'cleansed perception', when the usual 'measly trickle' of information from our surroundings becomes more of a steady flow.[57] I have already suggested that this would be a distinct disadvantage in the busy affairs of the world of becoming, but it might lead to new insights in a world of being.

Turning off technique. This technique seeks to restrict awareness of the outside world so that we may pay attention to the inner world of ideas and images. The problem is to avoid distraction not only from outside stimuli but also from unwanted thoughts. This is done by concentrating attention to a single unchanging source of stimulation or to a single unchanging image or idea. This could be a symbol such as the Cross, or the Star of David, or a mandala, either seen as a real object in front of the meditator on which he gazes, or a visual image held in the mind's eye. Sometimes the meditator is advised to gaze at a steady light or a candle flame, or to listen to a simple tune played over and over, or to the rhythmic sound of a gong or drum. Sometimes he repeats some word or phrase either aloud to himself or silently in his mind's ear. The stimulus may be a bodily movement repeated again and again in the form of a dance. Whatever it is, the stimulus is simple, mono-tonous and repeated over and over. Often it has little or no intrinsic meaning to the meditator, but serves to restrict his attention and divert it from the outward world of sense or the internal world of intrusive or unwanted thoughts.

This particular technique is similar to certain methods of inducing trance states, and may indeed do so in certain cases. However the goal is not apparently to put the meditator into trance, but to induce a mental state in which non-linear thinking becomes more possible with its promise of insight and fruitful re-orientation or patterning of ideas.

Quaker worship

Since Friends place unique value on the Quaker meeting for worship, it will now be important to discuss the relevance of what has gone before. For the sake of those readers who are not familiar with this form of religious practice, I must describe briefly what is likely to happen at a typical Quaker meeting.

The meeting for worship is held on a basis of silence, and any spoken contribution arises out of the silence, and the meeting returns to its silent worship after the contribution is over. Friends will gather for the meeting shortly before the appointed time and sit quietly in the meeting house or room where the meeting is to be held. This, of course, could be anywhere, as long as there is little to distract or interrupt the meeting. First there is the stage of quiet waiting, during which the meeting becomes 'gathered', and all become orientated to the business of worship and, sitting silently, try to leave behind them the concerns and worries of daily living. This stage may last about twenty minutes or so, during which many will sit with closed eyes and bowed heads. The first spoken contribution, which may come from anyone, young or old, experienced or quite new to the meeting, will often set the theme for later additions which will expand, develop, modify or add to what has gone before. People rarely, if ever, speak more than once at any given meeting. Sometimes new themes are introduced which may not be obviously relevant to what has already been said. If this happens, a contribution towards the end of the meeting may gather up the threads of previous themes and show how they all fit into a pattern. When this happens it is usual to let the meeting end in silence without anything more being said.

These vocal contributions to the meeting in no way constitute a debate or argument, or even a discussion. They are more like components added one by one to a pattern of ideas which develops during the meeting. Indeed, a logical discursive mode of thinking would seem entirely out of place. Instead, the non-linear consciousness described by Robert Ornstein is more appropriate to this kind of group meditation, leading to new and often unexpected insights.

This kind of group can only operate successfully if there is a strict discipline within that group, and a complete willingness of each individual to subordinate his needs to those of the group. It does not matter who speaks at meeting, it is what is said that is important. An individual contributor to the meeting does not, as it were, inject his own personal ideas into the meeting, but rather the exercise of the meeting calls out the contribution from him or her, because it is that contributions which is needed at that moment. This is reflected in the not uncommon experience in meeting of the same contribution being in the minds of more than one Friend, so that it does not matter which of them gets up and makes it, provided that it is made.

The conditions under which Quaker meetings are held would seem ideal for the turning off kind of concentrative meditation which I have been describing. Although concentrated attention on some external thing in the way described by Evelyn Underhill, may lead the worshipper to see the flowers on the table in a new way or to become entranced with the play of light on the wood graining of the floor, it seems more usual for there to be a withdrawal from external stimulation, in the quiet, familiar, unchanging surroundings of the meeting house. In addition to closing their eyes, Friends may repeat silently a suitable phrase to themselves, in order to still the surge of unwanted thoughts. Each has his or her method of 'centring down'. This may lead to a change in the manner of thinking and feeling. Just as vocal contributions may develop an overall pattern, so may ideas occurring to the individual in these circumstances. Thoughts form a new 'gestalt', a fresh emphasis, and familiar ideas may be entertained and experienced in quite a new way.

George Gorman in a former Swarthmore Lecture *The Amazing Fact of Quaker Worship* quotes a good description of this change in the manner of thinking:

> As I get nearer to the point of rising to speak, not only does my heartbeat rise (as you say, not a trustworthy sign of the Holy Spirit at work), but I have a mounting sense of mental activity—real excitement: thoughts colliding, falling into a moving pattern, joining to make new sense.

The Inner Light becomes almost a physical reality: it flickers over the content of the mind—and by mind I mean the whole content of both feelings and thoughts—and then comes to rest in a way that lights up the whole: so that on some rare occasions the statement I am about to make is presented to me whole, and I don't have to make my way through phraseology; it is 'given'.[58]

Many people would agree that the purpose of the meeting for worship is, as its name implies, primarily to worship God, although the term 'God' must have widely different meanings for different worshippers. In terms of this essay, it could fairly be said that the prime object of meeting for worship is to achieve a sense of glory: to ignore the busy world of becoming, and to pay attention for a while to the timeless world of being. In doing this our reverence, awe, admiration, love and wonder are awakened, and in theological parlance we 'worship God'.

There are, of course, additional spin-offs, to use a modern term, which accrue from group worship. Robert Barclay in a famous passage refers to the effect that meeting for worship had on him:

> . . . when I came into the silent assemblies of God's people, I felt a secret power among them, which touched my heart; and as I gave way unto it I found the evil weakening in me and the good raised up. . . . [59]

This is an experience to which most people could testify as being a valued result of worship and one which presumably enables us more effectively to be of use to others.

Another spin-off is one that concerns the achievement of insight and understanding which are found to have a direct relevance to, and influence on, the practical business of daily living and coping with problems and difficulties. In other words, insights from the world of being can influence what we do in the world of becoming. I have epitomized this by the phrase 'bringing the tablets down from Sinai', which is the title of the last chapter.

A Quaker meeting for worship, like other effective worship groups, develops a strong sense of identity and cohesion, just because it meets regularly with a common purpose of fundamental importance to its members. Besides providing the *milieu* and opportunity for achieving insight, the worshipping group provides a centre of friendship which serves as a reference point to which individual concerns can be brought and a secure base from which group action can be initiated.

VI

BRINGING THE TABLETS DOWN FROM SINAI

Anne Hayward has described what it is like to stand on Sinai:
> In a moment when I saw those hills properly I became
> conscious of a new awareness of life altogether and of
> love. I saw like a revelation, that up till then I had never
> really loved anything without expecting some return of
> love from it. And if the return did not come I would feel
> rejected. But now I could love those hills simply because
> they existed. I could love them in an infinite sort of way
> without wanting any return. It came to me then that this
> was real love and there need be no limit ever to whom or
> what I loved in this way. I was free to be happily in love
> with everyone in the world simply because they were there.[60]

This remarkable experience, an example of being-cognition,
has the characteristic feature of being self-validating, and
self-justifying. Such experiences have the character of ends
rather than means, to be worth having in and for themselves.
They seem to the experiencer to be what life is all about. Yet
we have to come down from Sinai, and the question now
remains whether we have anything to show for the experience,
other than the memory of it, and hopefully, a beneficent influence on our personality, outlook and behaviour. Do our peak-
experiences have to be justified by philanthropy and good works?

Western and Eastern attitudes to contemplation and good works
In our western culture there has been a tendency to admire
good works and to despise contemplation. Thomas Kelly put

it neatly when he said we have little time for those who stand gazing into the Great Beyond, because we have to hustle out to the garage and get the car in order to attend a special meeting on Christ and the Political Situation. Our protestant ethic, with its undertones of puritanism, steers us away from passive contemplation, perhaps just because it is so enjoyable, so rewarding. It seems so right to want to be busy helping those in trouble rather than to admire the sunset, to collect money for famine relief rather than to listen to a Beethoven symphony, to look out of our front doors to see what should be done next, rather than to enjoy the crisp morning air. We prefer talking to listening, teaching to learning, putting things to rights rather than letting things be. Our culture trains us to be busy and active, to make our mark, to stake our claim, to go out and win. Ambition anchors us to the world of becoming, predisposes us to perceive the world in the way best suited to meet our needs, or what we imagine to be the needs of others.

Our cultural training teaches us to control our environment, bend it to our will, make ourselves masters of it. The modes of Eastern thought, on the other hand, lead men to the notion of co-existence with nature. These contrasting attitudes may dispose each to its distinctive type of awareness: the Western to the purposeful, selective perception, tied to the goal of the moment; the Eastern to the more contemplative, appreciative, non-interfering awareness, less critical, more accepting, less selective, less busy. Eastern awareness does not attempt to make that curious break between the religious and the secular which is such a feature of Western thought with its dichotomy between the natural and the supernatural. The kind of secular religion or religious secularism of the East, specially that of Zen Buddhism, may have much to teach the West. Indeed it has affinities to Quakerism since it is a religion with no outward forms, which seeks an inculcation of a religious attitude without a need to formulate a creed. Quakers have always refused to make a division between the sacred and the secular.

The growing interest in meditation

Despite the emphasis on good works in our western culture, many religious people, especially in the Roman Catholic Church, have defended the contemplative, the poet, the dreamer and the mystic against the criticisms of the practical men of action. But the taste for contemplation has been restricted, at least in our western culture, to a minority. What is now so interesting is that this situation seems to be changing. There seems to be an increasing emphasis on the need for passive awareness as opposed to action. Evening classes on meditation, rare a few years ago, are now common and well-attended. New systems for developing the personality based on Yoga and other techniques are being taught. The emphasis seems less now on making 'ill' people well, as on helping people to develop their potential to the full. Our own young people are insisting that action is not enough. They are demanding something more than action and the fruits of action. They see ahead of them education and yet more education, training course after training course; nearly all designed to make them more effective men of action. Not surprisingly some are rebelling, opting out from the rat race, sometimes taking short cuts by experimenting with psychedelic drugs, or by joining hippy communities; but in the main seeking information and training in techniques which claim to produce new kinds of awareness and a development of their personalities.

The Quaker synthesis

Our own Society of Friends has, from the beginning, never been in any doubt about the need for contemplative awareness, for personal insights, and the need to seek these in private and corporate meditation and worship. The insistence of Friends that all members of the Society should attend meeting for worship regularly, reflects this view. It is important to note here that the Society of Friends has also been well aware of the dangers inherent in personal revelation of this kind. The history of religion is full of the records of prophets claiming a unique and infallible revelation. The hunches, openings, intuitions and bright ideas which we, as individuals, have from time to time, may be the real thing, but often they are not. It was to guard against the devil's promptings being taken for the voice of God, that institutional religions have produced a trained priesthood to advise, admonish and guide the laity. The Society of Friends has never had a priesthood. Instead, they have put the 'openings' of individuals within the context of the group. It is within the gathered meeting, as well as in personal devotions, that revelation is sought. When a Friend has an individual concern, he is expected to submit it to his meeting, and if it is considered by the meeting to be 'in right ordering' the Friend is encouraged to develop his concern with the support of the meeting. A balance has to be achieved on the one hand, between the 'individual concern' and the possibility of its being hare-brained and impractical, and on the other, the 'sense of the meeting' and the possibility of its being bigoted and reactionary. Whatever is decided, it is always important to detect and to support a genuine firsthand experience. William James has a wonderful passage in *The Varieties of Religious Experience*, dealing with just this point:

A genuine firsthand religious experience is bound to be a heterodoxy to its witnesses, the prophet appearing as a mere lonely madman. If his doctrine prove contagious enough to spread to any others, it becomes a definite and labelled heresy. But if it then still proves contagious enough

to triumph over persecution, it becomes itself an orthodoxy, and when a religion has become an orthodoxy
its day of inwardness is over: the spring is dry; the
faithful live at secondhand exclusively and stone the
prophets in their turn.[61]

It is the danger of living by stale, secondhand orthodoxies
that we must guard against. In the terminology of this essay,
the world of being has to inform and inspire the world of
becoming, and we have to learn to take the insights of the one
into the activity of the other.

Blueprint for action

Ideally then, action should stem from an initial, quiet,
contemplative appraisal of the situation by the individual or
by the group. This reduces the risk of hasty or blinkered action
stemming from personal desire, ambition or prejudice.
Decisions have to be arrived at in the sort of circumstances
conducive to non-linear thinking which, being out of time, is
not so likely to be shaped by the needs of the moment. Clearly
this method would be impractical for many of the decisions we
have to make in daily living and for which indeed such a
method would be quite inappropriate. But for many important
matters about which far-reaching decisions have to be made,
the contemplative, non-linear approach would seem to be the
more appropriate. This way of doing things has served to
re-orientate the Society of Friends away from an exclusive
concern with getting things done, and has earned the Society
too often the criticism of being unwilling to act quickly and
efficiently in matters of urgent concern. Nevertheless, in spite
of this, perhaps almost because of it, the Society has managed
to be quietly effective in a number of important concerns at
home and overseas.

Since our protestant ethic calls for action, we tend to ask

'What can be done tomorrow morning about it?' However, if the thesis of this essay is broadly correct, we should perhaps be asking: 'Ought I to interfere? *Dare* I interfere?' The situation or person may well be in need of our help, but we may not always know the best way to give it. Perhaps our initial response should be 'How can I understand?' rather than 'What can I do?' This calls for the loving, uncritical, accepting awareness of being-cognition, rather than the busy, interfering, desiring awareness of deficiency-cognition. Initially, the situation or person in need may be better served by the passive approach of being-cognition and non-linear consciousness, which, being for the moment out of time, lacks the insistent call for action *now*, which may so distort our view of the problem. Seen thus, the criminal does not cry out to be reformed, the alcoholic to be cured, the atheist to be converted. It is our loving, uncritical acceptance which may be called for in the first instance, undistorted by our desire to put him right, to have him conform to *our* notion of desirable behaviour or correct belief, or to do him good. We may then be better placed to discover what the most effective action might be, and how best we can serve him. In doing so we may come to realize how much *he* can help *us*.

There are times when we have to deal with the urgent needs of the moment, and seem to have time for nothing else. Each short term goal follows closely after the one before, so that we feel imprisoned by the pressure of events which seem to trap us and dictate our actions. But we can and must break free and seek the sort of vision which takes matters out of time and into a wider context. We shall then respond, not only to the dictates of immediate circumstance, but also in the light of those deeper insights we achieve when we realize that 'the burning bush has been kindled in our midst, and we stand together on holy ground'.

REFERENCES

[1] Read (Herbert) *The Contrary Experience: Autobiographies*. London: Secker & Warburg, 2nd edn., 1973.

[2] Nickalls (J. L.) ed., *The Journal of George Fox*. London: Cambridge University Press, 1952, p. 11.

[3] Aveling (Francis) *Personality and Will*. London: Cambridge University Press, 1931.

[4] Kee (Alistair) *The Way of Transcendence*. London: Penguin, 1971.

[5] Macmurray (John) *The Structure of Religious Experience*. London: Faber, 1936.

[6] *Exodus*, iii, 1–6 (NEB).

[7] Kelly (Thomas R.) *Reality of the Spiritual World* (1942) and *The Gathered Meeting* (1941). London: Friends Home Service Committee, 1965.

[8] Eddington (Arthur) *The Nature of the Physical World*. London: Cambridge University Press, 1928.

[9] Huxley (Aldous) *The Doors of Perception*. London: Chatto and Windus, 1954.

[10] James (William) *The Varieties of Religious Experience*. London: Longmans, 1962.

[11] Curle (Adam) *Mystics and Militants*. London: Tavistock, 1972.

[12] Maslow (Abraham H.) *Motivation and Personality*. New York: Harper, 1954.

[13] Maslow (Abraham H.) *Toward a Psychology of Being*. New York: Van Nostrand, 1962.

[14] Jones (Rufus) *Interpretation of Quakerism*. London: Friends Home Service Committee, 1948.

[15] Nickalls, *op. cit.*, p. 263.

[16] Collier (Howard) *The Quaker Meeting*. London: Friends Home Service Committee, 1949.

[17] Waddell (Helen) *The Desert Fathers*. London: Constable, 1936.

[18] Bannister (Roger) *First Four Minutes*. London: Putnam, 1955.

[19] Koestler (Arthur) *The Sleepwalkers*. London: Penguin, 1959.

[20] de Bono (Edward) *The Use of Lateral Thinking*. London: Penguin, 1967.

[21] Hudson (Liam) *Contrary Imaginations*. London: Penguin, 1966.

[22] Ornstein (Robert) *The Psychology of Consciousness*. London: Freeman, 1972.

[23] Heard (Gerald) *Training for the Life of the Spirit*. London: Cassell, 1941.

[24] Thompson (Francis) *The Hound of Heaven*. Oxford: Mowbray, 1947.

[25] Hans Denck quoted by Rufus Jones in *Spiritual Reformers in the 16th and 17th Centuries*. London: Macmillan, 1914.

[26] Toynbee (Arnold) *A Study of History*. London: Oxford University Press, 1954.

[27] Smart (Ninian) *The Religious Experience of Mankind*. London: Collins (Fontana), 1969.

Adam Curle

g Adam richard
Fill in Hingham

[28] Laski (Marghanita) *Ecstasy*. London: Cresset, 1961.

[29] Curle, *op. cit.*

[30] Maslow (Abraham H.) *Religions, Values and Peak-Experiences*. Ohio State University Press, 1964.

[31] Laski, *op. cit.*

[32] *Ibid.*

[33] Jefferies (Richard) *The Story of my Heart*. London: Macmillan, 1883.

[34] Collier, *op. cit.*

[35] James, *op. cit.*

[36] Snow (C. P.) *The Search*. London: Macmillan, 1934.

[37] 'The experience of John Wilhelm Rowntree, 1894' related by Rufus Jones and quoted in *Christian Faith and Practice in the Experience of the Society of Friends*. London Yearly Meeting of the Religious Society of Friends, 1960, § 472.

[38] Laski, *op. cit.*

[39] Huxley, *op. cit.*

[40] Thomas Traherne (1638–1674) quoted by Marghanita Laski in *Ecstasy, op. cit.*

[41] Kelly, *op. cit.*

[42] James, *op. cit.*

[43] Underhill (Evelyn) *Mysticism*. London: Methuen, 1911.

[44] Ornstein (Robert E.) *On Experience of Time*. London: Penguin, 1969.

[45] Laski, *op. cit.*

[46] Eliot (T. S.) 'Burnt Norton' in *Four Quartets*. London: Faber, 1944.

[47] Laski, *op. cit.*

[48] Underhill, *op. cit.*

[49] Laski, *op. cit.*

[50] Pointing (Horace B.) in *The Friend*, 19 June, 1964.

[51] Hesse (Hermann) *Narziss and Goldmund*. London: Penguin, 1959.

[52] Makins (Peggy) in a BBC radio broadcast, 12 December 1974.

[53] James, *op. cit.*

[54] Maslow, *Religions, Values and Peak-Experiences, op. cit.*

[55] Naranjo (J.) and Ornstein (R. E.) *On the Psychology of Meditation*. London: Allen & Unwin, 1972.

[56] Ornstein, *The Psychology of Consciousness, op. cit.*

[57] Huxley, *op. cit.*

[58] Gorman (George H.) *The Amazing Fact of Quaker Workship*. London: Friends Home Service Committee, 1973.

[59] Barclay (Robert) *An Apology for the True Christian Divinity* . . . 1676, quoted in *Christian Faith and Practice, op. cit.*, §41.

[60] Hayward (Anne) in *Woman's Hour* edited by Mollie Lee. London: BBC Publications, 1967.

[61] James, *op. cit.*